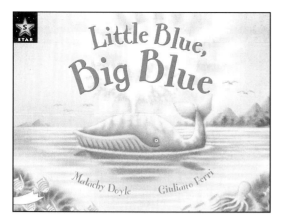

## The front cover

What do you think the story is about? (*a blue whale*)

Where is the story set? (*prompt for the word 'ocean'*)

What other animals live in the ocean?

## The back cover

The blurb on the back cover gives some clues about the story.

What sort of life might a baby blue whale have?

Do you think it will have any enemies?

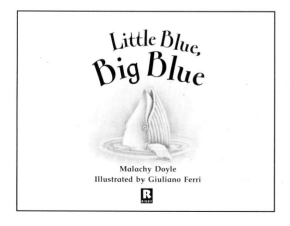

## The title page

Let's read the title again.

These are the names of the author, the illustrator and the publisher.

1

*Lesson 1 (Chapter 1)*

**READ**

# Read pages 2 to 5

*Purpose:* To find out about Little Blue's birth.

**PAUSE**

# Pause at page 5

Where is Little Blue born? What does he feed on? Where does he spend the winter? Where are the blue whales' feeding grounds? How long is it since Little Blue's mother had eaten?

Point out how much factual information about blue whales is contained in the text.

What does the map show you?

### Chapter 1

Little Blue was born in the warm seas near the equator. His mother pushed him to the surface of the water. Little Blue squealed as he took his first breath of air.

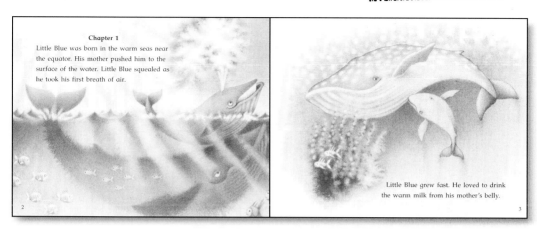

2

Little Blue grew fast. He loved to drink the warm milk from his mother's belly.

3

All winter long, Little Blue stayed close to his mother and she taught him many things. Little Blue loved to play beside her in the water. He loved to stretch his head above the water to breathe in the salty air.

4

Soon it was time to swim north for the summer, to the feeding grounds. It had been many months since Little Blue's mother had eaten, and she was very hungry.

It was a long way to the polar waters in the north.

RUSSIA    ALASKA, U.S.A.

CANADA

5

**READ**

# Read pages 6 to 9

*Purpose:* To find out about Little Blue and his mother's journey to the northern feeding grounds.

**PAUSE**

# Pause at page 9

Why do blue whales come up to the surface?

What do blue whales eat?

How do they eat the krill? How many krill are there in a blue whale's mouthful? What words describe the krill? (*tiny, pink*)

Further and further they swam. They came up to the surface every few minutes to breathe. Little Blue loved to spout water vapour high in the air.

6

Finally, they reached the polar waters in the north. The sea felt cold to Little Blue, but he did not mind. His mother showed him how to eat the tiny pink krill that swarmed all around them.

7

Little Blue's mother opened her mouth wide and took a great big gulp. Water flowed in, carrying thousands of krill. Then she pushed out the water with her tongue and swallowed the food.

8

Little Blue did the same. The tiny krill tasted good.

9

**READ**

# Read pages 10 and 11

*Purpose:* To find out about an enemy of the blue whale.

**PAUSE**

# Pause at page 11

Who has attacked Little Blue?

Who is able to drive the killer whales away?

What word describes a group of killer whales? (*pod*)

What sort of story is this? (Children need to notice that it is like an information story.)

*Please turn to page 15 for Revisit and Respond activities.*

One day, Little Blue was busy feeding when a pod of killer whales appeared. They swam around him, nipping him with their sharp teeth. Little Blue cried out in fear.

At once his mother was beside him. She lashed the killer whales with her tail and drove them away. Little Blue stayed close to his mother after that.

11

*Lesson 2 (Chapter 2)*

**RECAP**

## Recap lesson 1

Where was Little Blue born?

Where do Little Blue and his mother swim to for summer?

What did they eat?

What is the enemy of the blue whale?

**READ**

## Read pages 12 to 15

*Purpose:* To find out how Little Blue changes.

**PAUSE**

## Pause at page 15

How has Little Blue become Big Blue?

What keeps Big Blue warm in the cold polar waters?

What has happened to Big Blue's mother?

Why could Big Blue get trapped?

Where does Big Blue need to swim to?

What word describes the call of the whales? (*lonely*)

## Chapter 2

As summer went on, Little Blue grew and grew. He was not little anymore. A thick layer of blubber had grown under his skin because of all the krill he had eaten.

Now he was Big Blue, one of the largest creatures on Earth.

Soon summer became winter, and the polar waters turned cold. Big Blue's blubber kept him warm, but every day there was less to eat. The krill began hiding under the ice.

One day Big Blue went to look for his mother, but he could not find her. She had left him to look after himself, for he was big enough now. Big Blue swam in great circles in the freezing waters, but there were no other whales to be found. Where had they gone? The sea was turning to ice, and Big Blue was in danger of becoming trapped.

Down went Big Blue, under the ocean, to see if it was warmer there. That's when he heard the lonely call of the whales. It came through the sea from far, far away.

"Swim south," it said. "Swim south, before the waters freeze!"

**READ**

# Read pages 16 to 19

*Purpose:* To find out about Big Blue's journey south.

**PAUSE**

# Pause at page 19

Where is Big Blue swimming to?

Is Big Blue frightened? How would you would feel if you had to go on a journey on your own? What could happen to him? Look back in the text for clues.

Big Blue swam for two months – what do you think that would be like?

What do you think is about to happen?

"I'm coming!" sang Big Blue, "I'm coming!"
He turned his back on the ice
and snow. He turned his back on
the seals and the polar bears.
    Big Blue started swimming
towards the warmer waters of
the equator.
    Up and down his tail
thrashed. Left and right his
flippers turned, as he swam
through the ocean.
    Big Blue swam for two whole
months without seeing another
blue whale.

16

17

    One day, he saw several shadows in the distance.
Were they blue whales like him? Big Blue swam
quickly towards the shadows, calling out to them
with excitement. But the shadows did not answer
in a language he understood.

18

    Big Blue lifted his head above the surface
of the sea. What he saw filled him with fear.
The shadows were not other blue whales.
They were the shadows of his enemies,
the killer whales.

19

**READ**

# Read pages 20 and 21

*Purpose:* To find out if Big Blue escapes from the killer whales.

**PAUSE**

# Pause at page 21

How do you think Big Blue felt hiding from the killer whales?

How did he defeat them? How did he learn that?

**READ**

# Read pages 22 to the end

*Purpose:* To find out where in the ocean is home for Big Blue.

Big Blue stopped swimming and stayed silent. He hoped the black-and-white whales had not seen or heard him. His mother was not here to protect him now.

Big Blue took his biggest breath and swam down, deep down under the water. He stayed there for as long as he could. Big Blue felt very frightened and very alone.

After a while, the shadows moved on, and Big Blue decided to continue his journey. Suddenly, without warning, a pair of killer whales came at him. Big Blue called out for help, and began thrashing his tail like his mother had done.

Big Blue and the killer whales fought a great battle. Finally, the killer whales swam away to join the rest of their pod. Big Blue had won.

Big Blue started swimming south again. He was more careful now. Every now and then, he heard a sound travelling through the sea. It was the sound of other blue whales, telling him where to go. Big Blue answered back and swam even faster.

After a time, the waters began to feel warmer on Big Blue's skin. He knew that he was getting closer to the equator. Big Blue squealed with happiness.

At last, Big Blue reached the warm, calm seas near the equator. He could finally rest among the other blue whales. Big Blue stopped swimming and basked in the sun and the warm water.

"I'm home," he sang. "Home at last."

24

**PAUSE**

# Pause at page 24

What phrase tells you Big Blue is very happy? (*Big Blue squealed with happiness*, page 23)

What word describes what Big Blue does when he stops swimming? (*basked*)

# After Reading

## Revisit and Respond

### Lesson 1

**T** Ask the children to list all the information they find out about blue whales, e.g. *what they eat, where they feed,* etc.

**T** Ask the children what they can remember about the book *Mantu the Elephant* (Gold level) by the same author, Malachy Doyle. (Have copies of the book available if possible.) Discuss similarities and differences.

### Lesson 2

**T** Using the book for information, ask each child in a group to compile a quiz of five questions about blue whales to ask the other members of their group. They could take turns to ask questions.

**T** Continue to compare the story with *Mantu the Elephant.* What happens in the second half of both stories? Discuss common themes, e.g. *a battle, learning about life, happiness with herd/school.*

**T** Ask the children to make a list of the factual information in the story (e.g. blue whale surfacing to breathe). Ask the children to make a list of the fictional information in the story (e.g. Big Blue's adventures and feelings).

**W** Ask the children to look through the book and make a list of words related to a whales' life, e.g. *krill, pod, basked, blubber.*

# Follow-up

## Independent Group Activity Work

This book is accompanied by two photocopy masters, one with a reading focus, and one with a writing focus, which support the main teaching objectives of this book. The photocopy masters can be found in the Planning and Assessment Guide.

**PCM 57** (*reading*)

**PCM 58** (*writing*)

## Writing

**Guided Writing:** Look at the similarities and differences between *Little Blue, Big Blue* and *Mantu the Elephant*. Use PCM 58.

**Extended Writing:** Using the information in the story, write what happened to Big Blue next.

# Assessment Points

*Assess that the children have learnt the main teaching points of the book by checking that they can:*

- identify similarities and differences between the stories of Malachy Doyle
- point out features of this author's style
- pick out factual information from the text.